unidentified domestic object

unidentified domestic object

poems by

Heather Newman

© 2026 Heather Newman. All rights reserved.
This material may not be reproduced in any form, published,
reprinted, recorded, performed, broadcast,
rewritten or redistributed without
the explicit permission of Heather Newman.
All such actions are strictly prohibited by law.

Cover design by Shay Culligan
Cover image by Debbie Galant
Author photo by Heather Newman

ISBN: 979-8-90146-902-6

Kelsay Books
502 South 1040 East, A-119
American Fork, Utah 84003
Kelsaybooks.com

For my mother

who believed

and my father

who dreamed

Acknowledgments

Thank you to the following publications, where versions of these poems previously appeared:

Aji Magazine: "Bourbon Street, 3 AM"
Barrow Street 4 x 2: "Perception"
Entropy Magazine: "Sing-a-Long," "A 1980 Cruise"
Hanging Loose Magazine: "Dreaming in French," "Aging," "Survival," "I lost"
Hole in the Head Review: "do-mes-tic," "object"
How to Love the World (Storey Publishing): "Missing Key"
The Inquisitive Eater: "Tradition"
Love's Executive Order: "Pandemic Pantoum for a Circuitous Life"
Matter: "Stumped"
MoonPark Review: "The Hidden Masterpiece Behind Miss Amy's Confirmation and a New Genre of Performance Art"
New Verse News: "This Time" renamed "Common Shooting"
NJ Bards Review: "The Tryst," "To Nail Polish"
The Pi Review: "unidentified"
The Potomac—A Journal of Poetry & Politics: "Unconventional Sonnet from a Party Girl"
Right Hand Pointing: "wild canary"
Voices From Here (Paulinskill Press): "Searching for Light in the Lunar Eclipse"
The Wisconsin Review: "How They Remember"
Writers Circle Anthology: "MIA"

Thank you to esteemed poets David Lehman and Elaine Equi. It was an honor to study with you at The New School. Special thanks to the editors of Hanging Loose Press for giving this latecomer a chance. Loving thanks to Fran Schumer and the NJ-5 (Caprice Garmin, Ruchama Feuerman, Julie Sloan) for helping me find my voice. I am grateful for the feedback from the (former) South Mountain Poets, especially Marcia LeBeau, Robin Rosen Chang, Patricia Runkle, David Stanford Burr, and Judith Christian.

Bravo to the superb poets whose workshops inspire. You are my creative lifeline: James Crews, Neil Shepard, and the Pat Carlin group—Leah Umansky, Susan Bruce, Wendy Weinstein, Bergen Hutaff, Beth Dufford, Suze Bienaimee, Sarah Paley. Shout-outs to book cover artist, Debbie Galant, my Summit book club (Page Turners—over 30 years!) and Create & Connect at Christ Church.

Cheers to my beloved friends who keep me hiking, biking, swimming and smiling: Melanie, Cathy, Moira, Deb, Dana, Julia, Kathy, Dara, Mary, Laurie, Fran, Marie, Tracy, Pam F., Heidi H., Helen, Allison, Christie, Rhoda, Barb, Ava, Pam P., Carole, Denise, Julie A., Donna, Heidi B., Robin, Patty, Amy, Julie B., and the amazing All On cyclists.

Above all, I am grateful for my family. I love you all. Jon, you support my creative endeavors and endure my burning of the bread. Thank you, thank you, for all that you do. Matt, your energy and humor are endearing, number one son. Thanks for explaining AI to me. (You understand I'm just trying to do laundry.) Julia, your kindness is a gift, and your talent is the bomb. Dearest daughter, write your story, play your song. Carry on! To Macintosh marvels Mom, Dad, Randy, and Colin, thank you for applauding my early musings. And to Michele, Liza, Ira, Amy, Brian and newcomers Reilly and Jack—what a great village.

Contents

Dreaming in French	13
Survival	14
What Holds	15
Pandemic Pantoum for a Circuitous Life	16
Searching for Light in the Lunar Eclipse	17
Safekeeping	18
Perception	20
How They Remember	21
Aging	22
Numb	23
unidentified	24
do-mes-tic	25
object	27
Tradition	28
Deal Breakers	29
The Tryst	30
Natural Partners	32
I lost	35
wild canary	36
Insomnia	37
Creation	40
Libation	42
Bourbon Street, 3 AM	44
Jealous	45
Please Tell Me I'm Hipper Than My Algorithm	47
Sing-along	48
don't rant	49
THE HIDDEN MASTERPIECE BEHIND MISS AMY'S CONFIRMATION AND A NEW GENRE OF JUDICIAL PERFORMANCE ART	51

Stumped	55
My Body in This Term	56
Common Shooting	57
this is what we mean by blue	59
The Cardiologist	60
Unconventional Sonnet from a Party Girl	61
A 1980 Cruise	62
To Nail Polish	64
MIA	65
Colonizer	66
Missing Key	67

Dreaming in French

I'm driving this huge school bus of kids down the steep Rue Lepic
wedged between the steering wheel and the windshield. I can't
reach the pedals, have no way to accelerate or stop.
      It is raining in Montmartre.
I am barreling down at high speeds as my derrière steers
allowing me to veer off into red-light alleys,
      How very French.
The kids are cheering my cinematic misses with cars
which might be funny if it didn't feel so real.
      Freud says I am both the bus and the driver.
I say it's sheer terror.
      Freud says I am the kids, the rain and even the wheel.
I say it's drama with comic relief.
      We both say I am out-of-control pedals.
Ahead I see my little dog, a white Coton de Tulear.
He is stuck in the back of a garbage truck about to be crushed
to death even as his tail keeps wagging.
      I am the royal dog of Madagascar.
I jump out of the bus to rescue him, my instincts
to growl and bite and lick as fierce as a runaway bus.
      Freud says it's my superego protecting me.
      I say I wouldn't dream of running away.

Survival

Adorning herself with yellowjackets
she beelines a trail from hip to hip,
egg to egg, star of every sting.
Colonies, pheromones, swarms

she would never settle for a hole
in the frame of a sliding door.
She could chew her way out of any cell.
But now

assessing the hive, dragging her abdomen as she goes.
She might live this way a few more years,
high-pitched chirps, the occasional drone.
It's not that she's wrecked from mating

She suffers the plight of every femme fatale:
eat or be eaten.

What Holds

The memory of those early years sticks
like candle wax to a tablecloth. Crystal stems,
heirloom silver, an embarrassment of riches,
my mother would say. An evening breeze sprinkles
wax without notice. Perhaps we were all drunk.
Still, pearly remnants remain wash after wash.
I've folded too many tablecloths to recall
the particular night when I stopped caring.
The shame's in the memory of the struggle.
The will to make a home perfect. Labor
over a new recipe, racing out for butter
to create a proper roux. This is the rub of guilt.
It takes as much effort to scour a stain
as it does to watch the oil and wax melt away.

Pandemic Pantoum for a Circuitous Life

after Terrance Hayes

I lock you in an American colonial that is part God-fearing,
part insomnia, a cul-de-sac of hijacked aspiration.
I lock you in a quatrain that is two-part harmony, two-
part wishbone to remove from a chicken and fight over

Part insomnia, a cul-de-sac of hijacked aspiration
I deliver you from Amazon Prime
a wishbone to remove from a chicken and fight over,
Lock your evil mower, there are unmasked children in the yard

I deliver you from Amazon Prime
both a planter for seeds and voyeur of trees,
Lock your evil mower, there are unmasked children in the yard
(circle walks his rhetoric another chardonnay)

Both a planter for seeds and voyeur of trees,
As the planter, you raise schools of petals in a broom closet
(circle walks his rhetoric another chardonnay)
As voyeur, *that soon we may touch, love, explain*

Planter, you raise schools of petals in a broom closet
locked in belief that anything is possible,
Voyeur, *that soon we may touch, love, explain*
enough to come home to roost

Locked in belief that anything is possible
you dream up your Malaysian get-a-way,
It is not enough to come home to roost,
It is not enough to love art, you must live it

Searching for Light in the Lunar Eclipse

I look to the sky and beg,
"reveal yourself,"
and I will ask no more than the shift of a gray cloud,
a glimpse of red sky to illuminate my view,
if only this rare blood moon would show true color.
You, I ask, is that you, old man on the moon
flashing through scattered clouds
gleaming slivers
what, hope? did you mean hope?
Another cloud passes,
a nighthawk circles overhead.
In the distance a curdled honk
what, his forlorn mate, or a clumsy saxophone?
I long for revelation to jazz my blues, anything
more than hand puppet clouds
fingering shadows on my dark lawn
stirring the base of my soul
what, another dark soul?
redundant as a super eclipse shrouded in hazy skies
leaving unidentified hues, blues, gray matter
in the ozone,
relegating moonlight
to lyrics

Safekeeping

The herd has arrived but I notice them one at a time.
Doe eyes searching, they hoof single file through the snow.

You can seek asylum here I say aloud, remembering
the last time I spotted deer in my yard. I held Lancelot in my arms.
My sweet dog of twelve years had heart failure and it was a matter
of hours. This was all before I thought about refugees, before
I was sickened by TV news, before creatures jumping over fences
and walls made my heart jump, such desperate acts once reserved
for hungry deer. Back then I believed the deer had come
for Lancelot. Reincarnation! Now my thoughts race to my father
in memory care.

Are you here for Dad?

I want to believe that the large buck walking toward my window
is a messenger. The others scatter, finding new rhododendron.
One even settles down to rest in a sunny spot. But this bold buck
makes eye contact.

If you're here with a message, walk two steps closer.

I want to bargain for a safe haven.

Don't leave. You are welcome here.

I sit at a table in a house, in a neighborhood, in a town, in a state,
in a state of shock. *How does this happen?* You see one deer
and suddenly there's a herd. They have reason to gather and hide.

What the district states: local deer cull to revitalize the ecology.
Cull being the softer form of kill. Ecology being not a forest
or ecosystem but a small wood on the edge of prime suburban
real estate. A wood full of men with guns. Men with reasons, men
without reason.

I want to care less about dented car fenders or ravaged shrubs
or overpopulation.

The does and fawns have gathered around the stone birdbath.
On this winter morning, I seek asylum. I see a manger scene
and want to swaddle the world.

Perception

She found a job and hunkered down that winter, though
he had taken off to shoot volcanoes in Bora Bora.
She knew it signaled an exit strategy but signed on as

an underpaid assistant to a misogynist in a
windowless office. We say we pay for our fathers'
sins, meaning she paid off her husband's cell phone bill

with more unknown callers. In one version of truth,
the female rabbit pulls out her fur to add to the nest
as Daphne, now a tree, thanks Apollo for cutting her branches.

How They Remember

Here is a mother and her daughter,
the grandmother is seated at their table.
They drink to their generations,
the girl, organic coffee in a reusable cup

the grandmother is seated at their table
drinking her tea from Wedgewood bone,
the girl, organic coffee in a reusable cup
the mother, reticent, sips gin

drinking her tea from Wedgewood bone
grandmother regales the girl with stories
the mother, reticent, sips gin,
but I want to hear *your* stories, mom

grandmother regales the girl with stories
as mother recalls things differently,
but I want to hear *your* stories, mom,
so she talks and talks or was it the gin

as mother recalls things differently
the daughter becomes angry
so she talks and talks or was it the gin
that poisoned the way she remembers things

the daughter becomes angry,
she wants the real story, what happened
that poisoned the way she remembers things,
how they drink to their generations.

Aging

We give it little thought until it's all we think about,
thousands of little thoughts breaching evening dreams.
Ancestral beds of soft yarn, strong DNA, waste,
of difficult men going rogue,
of sweet men going mad. I awake each night
precisely at four. Rather, it's my dawn.
Drowning out mourning doves 'til six.
In those stark hours I think about death

How it would feel to lay in a coffin, my animal spirit
the red-tailed hawk, gliding peacefully above.
I list all the ones I love, in order of importance,
and wish for them. Not prayers, exactly.
Give her peace and security. Help him let go.
Until I spot my rabbit.

Numb

Tossing in a fitful sleep
I turn my back but cannot reach
out—what was that dream that startled me?
I've slept on my arm and compressed my blood flow

Like origami my tender limb tissues
fold and open, create a valley, cross a line.
I clutch this dream in my fist until it fades
as my arm comes back to life

So much is held in my maternal arm,
this arm that once soothed and held my son

Gone, my tingling pain is gone
and this is not the trauma of a lost limb,
it is the temporary effect of
being cut off, losing sensation
remedied by going through the motions,
circulation, rotation, activation,
bearable distractions

while vibrations hum in my chamber,
what he said, *hmmm,* what I said, *hmmm,*
what I should have said, *hmmm*

These vocal, cerebral, aortic phenomena
resonate like some rare, nocturnal cancer
forgiven   by the clean swipe of dawn

unidentified

not whipped not buttercream
some white filler

fugitive dust
         a meandering Jane Doe
he she it they   trap door
       pseudonyms

lost monoxide
unculturable bacteria

riding the delta wave

read my faceless
         lips unknown

 Adermatoglyphia

     the way they mutate
        among us

do-mes-tic

Used as an adjective, the word relates to the running
of a home or to family relations, such as a domestic
chore, domestic service or domestic worker

but when used as a noun, she (preferred pronoun) is that person
paid/or unpaid to help out with menial tasks such as cleaning
and cooking and scrubbing and ironing and mending and when
expanded, domestic can mean more than a helper or homemaker,
indigenous species or quiet pleasure, domestic can mean
in charge of a household, even *lady of the house*

Defined on a broader scale, she is neither foreign nor international,
she exists or occurs inside a particular country;
for example: *the current state of domestic affairs;*
or in simpler terms, she is a product not made abroad

Synonyms for domestic abound: maid, housemaid,
maid-of-all-work, charwoman, charlady, char, daily,
daily woman, skivvy, scullion, and (the preferred term
used at country clubs) Mrs. Mop

Used as a verb: she *domesticates* a lion in the wild,
she *domesticates* the cubs in their den,
she makes them fond of, and good at, home life
and all the tasks it involves

Placement of domestic in word order should not be confused
with world order, dominance or domination
is reserved for the he: he is male, boy or animal;
he stands for *H E* as in High Explosive, High Efficiency,
His Eminence, His Excellency

He (replacement for God) is used in most grammatical situations
while *she* is used for boats and ships, the female symbol
pertaining to vessels or wombs, and much like the domestic,
her function is to contain: *She is one fine vessel.*

On a side note, domestic nouns (male/female/other?) can
be contained or concealed in containers on domestic
and international waters; *They* who lack documentation
or channels to a mother ship can be cause for muddied
waters, bordering on the illegal

Of course, there are exceptions. In World War II,
the German battleship *Bismarck* was regarded
as being so magnificent that it was described
using male terms, but back to the colloquial
do-mes-tic and why

it's no longer up for interpretation

object

to be or not
to be that thing
that ring
that-a-girl
easy does it

is animal instinct
the thing to make
cat woman
sex kitten
ski bunny
a real dog

when the sky is falling
don't throw like a girl

man-made things
put a gun to your head

Tradition

First, the fork, then the knife, then the spoon.
Order, propriety, tradition.
Start left, it's like reading a book,
the blade turns in, the blade turns in
(easy to forget that one)
Fork. Then knife. Then spoon.
Three times a day. This reinforces
the way to set tables
and the way to hide under them,
under the fork, the knife, the spoon,
the fist on the table, the shattered glass
the shattered girl the shattered glass
girl turns left then right
the blade turns in, the blade turns in

Deal Breakers

My friend has left her husband of forty years
and we talk about guilt. We talk about the holes
that were left when she removed half the living room,
her etching on the hearth replaced by golf trophies.
New stockpiles of frozen dinners suggest evidence
of his laziness or ineptness or perhaps, like me, he simply
hates cooking. They were a couple in perpetual motion,
trading up homes, and nobody saw past the picket fence.
My friend refers to moving as her "real estate fix."

Why do people break? Some say marriage breaks down
over family, money, and sex. I think this is simplistic
but rhetoric loves the rule of three. Wise men, little pigs,
blind mice, bears, they all had their stories that led them down
a path. My friend had hers—location, location, location.

Troubles early-on become ever-after: the arguer, cheater,
narcissist, toxic labels of blame. Freud traces it back
to unresolved childhood conflict but my friend insists
that Freud is patriarchal and outdated. She just got tired
of working so hard. Diamonds last forever
but when a gem breaks loose from its setting, it's gone.

Is marriage a work of artful handling or a crapshoot? On the day
his divorce was final, my friend's husband shot a hole-in-one,
forcing the golf club to buy each member a round. This time
it was his break, the club's loss, and anyone's guess
how it goes around next time.

The Tryst

This is a tryst story.
It does not pretend
to be a love story.
It's a meeting of the body
in spite of the mind.
It is transparent,
a flimsy negligee,
a caress of the shoulder,
a minibar charge.
It knows its end
from the beginning,
justifies itself
when misunderstood.
It can be reserved
like a civil war love letter
or fall to cliché
like his, "You're dangerous,"
followed by her, "No, you are."
A tryst story plays rhyme games
like baby do the twist, resist my kiss,
oh please persist, get my gist?
It skips blank space.
Impetuous and explosive,
it tends to self-publish.

And if it happens to lounge
carelessly in a French bistro
on a busy corner in Manhattan
you can bet the joie de vivre
of your tête-à-tête
will turn quel dommage
much like the end
of a French noir film.

Natural Partners

I like to get personal with my trees
give a shout out to Gigantor
for standing strong against the range
shake a firm branch of Barnstopper

who blocks out the scene
even ancient willow Kai
is spared—we can't chop down
her indigenous spirit

as if naming trees would make them mine
I cursed a building that wasn't built
called it wrong, commercial, ugly
called it out for ruining my view

picture this: a quaint red barn
on acres of rolling farmland
green mountains in the distance
white steeple in the foreground

now: trucks and forklifts
promising new and improved
traffic patterns, green space
altered for the sake of profit

a sprawling hotel development
was planned for the forty-acre parcel
below my mountain
and I couldn't stand it, couldn't stop it

instead of looking right down the Massachusetts valley
I looked left at a white pine blocking my vista
instead of gazing up toward the snow-peaked range
I stared down the dirt in that forsaken field below

daydreamed about taking an axe
to the great pine, cutting it down to size
although the logic was missing I felt that
chopping a tree would set things right

true, it was never my valley to begin with
but it's easy to get attached to land
that goes further back than Paleo-Indians
who inhabited this self-seeding heaven

it gives one a sense of ownership
if you buy into the American dream—
I never thought I did
until I owned a home with a view

as it happens, the hotel never got built
never got its funding or something
had I known then that my fuss
would come to nothing, just like the build

I would have spent time listening to the wind
while sampling varieties of sap and bark
from those newly-named native trees
I would have searched for a nest in the thicket

an open cup of twigs, grass and weeds woven
into a three-way fork in an upright branch
I would have studied its sturdy construction
the impervious shield to rainstorms and snow

before begging those tiny nest-dwellers
tell me, please, how do you welcome
the next guest home?

I lost

my place in the Nocturne on the 20th bar

a parking spot at the mall

sunglasses keys one glove virginity

my one-track mind

eight tracts of nerves

a month to a hedonist

five pounds in the raw

myself in a threesome (unless I miscounted)

fourth-row center seats

sight of a fifth (ten for the road)

a timely sixth sense

all down a toilet

every single cause

my one shot

one kamikaze shot

the last call

wild canary

she was all barb and quip
that summer, quilling
their nest
while he hauled
the heavy twigs

to make matters worse
she liked to sing

Insomnia

I can't sleep because of a word beginning with E or I. Enigmatic? Iridescent? No.

"You're ____," he said, reducing me to a single word and I, sleepless and dulled by wine, forget. Irresistible? Impossible.

"Let's sit next to each other and heckle the MC." His eyes are wicked; the benevolent fundraiser our excuse to misbehave.

Guiding me across the massive ballroom to table six, he compliments my dress. Predictable. "You know you're one of my favorite people," he says.

I feel like pressing him on this. Out of how many? "I bet you say that to all your wife's friends."

I expect the usual fare after years of flirting; gossip over spicy tuna, innuendos screened behind sushi and a film for four.

He waves to a buddy, then turns back to me. "I learned about priorities in rehab. Life is too short." Just what is he saying? "There were many times I didn't feel like going out. But we'd go, and I'd realize it's not what you do, but who you're with."

"We're completely opposite," he continues. "I bottle it up, but you . . ." he gains momentum with each word, "you laugh, you bring out the best in me."

"Thanks, that's kind," I say, meaning it. He's my friend.

"But there's this tension . . ." He stops next to a table of gregarious men in tuxes and blonde, bejeweled ladies passing around a guidebook. It's time to sit down for dinner, the live auction is starting. "You're flamboyant," he says.

My raised brow says it all.

He searches for a better word. "You're E. Or I."

Who else but a frustrated writer in a perpetual midlife crisis would toss and turn over semantics? My inner actress embellishes the scene as mental cinematics become sexy. We glide across the dance floor, a blur of blue satin, while other guests disappear. Where is his wife, my friend, in all this? Shaking her head at the spectacle, or preoccupied like my husband?

At the table he whispers, "you're hot" or "so hot." Something was hot. So unlike him, a cool character who chooses words carefully. Perhaps I was mistaken. Maybe he said, "it's hot," referring to the soup.

Something has changed since he quit drinking. The rules of the game are fuzzy. I'm not sure he's playing anymore. My God, it was effervescent.

"You're effervescent."

So I'm a cross between a flamenco dancer and an Alka-Seltzer. Talk about chemistry: he, a bender-surviving, alpha male hell-bent on true confessions and I, a bubbly, wined up product of suburban monotony. Fission and fusion. Such spontaneous combustion could detonate even the deadliest carpool line.

I'm effervescent. No wonder I can't sleep.

Creation

I avoid adjectives,
rely on verbs
to excite
and nouns
to subject
my words
to scrutiny
by creators
in a room
around a table
who avoid malice,
rely on acumen
to subject
creations
to analysis
by reading into
meanings
out of context
mispronounced by
cretins
who developed technique
imitating
Greeks
whose words derived from
cavemen
who created language

to avoid
grunting
and relied on
words
to improve
procreation,
excite the women
and subject the men
to analysis
by reading into
meanings
out of context.

Libation

Welcome back Dionysus
you well-oiled fool
mingling music of the aulos
with rock and roll

luring this tipsy lady
to the edge of the cliff
to the brink of arsenic
on the rocks

clink! double over in ecstasy
dare you to jump
now watch your time
cut off at the wrist

It's a happy bleed
until it's not

Boots

on the ground no match
for these made-for-walkin'
kick-your-heels up spike-
high platform screamin'
agony of de-booty call all
I wanna do is have some
sun bitchin'
Santa Monica stride-
driven hot-for-stalkin'
smooth-talkin' boulevard
boots

No fatigue   no army   no march
or swagger   no strut or combat
no traipse   or step out
hightailin'
tootsies
spell

fit like Cinderella
hip like Jimmy Choo
red-soled Christian Louboutin
stylin' Manolo Blahnik

No waders or moonboots for me
Sir I'm a thigh-high ankle-bitin'
high ridin' Wellington girl
swoon rockin' on a slow tune
to China in my two-step
leg-up Fifth Avenue
boots

Bourbon Street, 3 AM

Somewhere between the sax and piano I lost my summer hat
forgot where I hung it
if I hung it

my new friend is on the next stool
I'm left with the horn player ordering his nightly shot
somewhere between notes he lost his place   improvised

play it again I say

outside it's a packed house skunked with tossed trash
hot Saturday studs saddled for action
I single out a plumed chapeau
loud proud a French peacock
turning heads strutting blue feathers
hell we're all winging it

play it again doesn't play this time   who says
I can't rock that peacock hat sidle up to anyone I choose
rather than flock to pretenders stumbling through birdland
   somewhere out there it's open-mic night

Here in the lonely corner the keyboardist
riffs off his syncopated tangent
   a mind away from the swaying ensemble
eyes fixed on a solo mix
his gray fedora tipped just a bit off center
enough to throw this whole set
    offkey

Jealous

after The Revenant

I am the teacher you called your mentor,
the poet you adored, coveted, eulogized,
come back to say this true thing:
I never liked your poetry—not one bit.

When I read your prize-winning work,
I longed for an interpreter.
When I attended your reading,
I thought of my piles of dirty laundry.

I resented your juxtapositions,
esoteric metaphors and pomposity,
your nods to Whitman, Yeats and Auden
as if they were somehow responsible.

I would have passed you along
but I counted on your fees,
my success memorialized
in your back-page acknowledgment.

I admit the rush of female prodigies
would entice me
but only because their trust
and their legs inspired me to write.

You'd like to think better of me
but the best I can do is come clean:
I hated my retirement party, the group gift,
disliked my editor and, worse, your boyfriend.

The smell of your perfume drove me mad.
You asked too many questions in class.
All I ever wanted was an hour
alone with you in my office.

While you wrote, I watched your
fine brow arch in surprise,
I imagined your gaping mouth
had I won the prize.

Now I am free of male-pattern baldness,
adjunct salaries, ex-wives,
the absurdity of beginner's luck,
and that is all you need to know about blue heaven

except what you may have heard
from romantics puffing in vain
that here, prolific poets use their Pushcarts
to pop their bonnets playing pushpin

Please Tell Me I'm Hipper Than My Algorithm

I'm grateful for local community forums
and Broadway-sponsored show reviews,
anything brought to you by *The New Yorker*
or brought to me by Uber Eats, but when I discover
Facebook Purity as a browser plug to remove my unwanted ads,
I am forced to separate good websites from the bad,
time-wasters from the true way I should bide my time.

After playing *Wordle*, I ponder headlines selected just for me.
 "Was the pandemic started by a lab leak or natural transmission?"
The evidence is laid out in two clear arguments,
and I am not surprised to learn that officials still remain divided.

If the CIA won't weigh in, what hope is there for me to separate
fact from fiction, camouflaged commercials from useful updates?
I feel pea brained, a digital *you are what you eat*.

I spend the morning removing annoying and irrelevant posts
with a mix of emotion: suspicious that Purity might
store my information, hopeful that fluff busting will work,
ashamed for caring so much about a profile. I curate my image
just to spend time cleaning up my act.

I am the tomato I just ate, confused about being a fruit
or a vegetable.

Sing-along

I'm invited to drink and sing around the piano.
I'm that standby you call when you need a lounge
act or reveler for the company Christmas bash.
There's a judge jamming on the Steinway, a scientist
who'd rather belt than study DNA, his ninety-five
year-old mother who looks twenty years younger,
and I tell her so. She corrects me. "Only twenty?"
My friend plays maestro and turns the pages of
sheet music, three sheets to the wind, a few bars
too early and the chorus gets sloppy. Not me.
Tonight I refrain which is the best part of a song.
Remember the refrain, I repeat to myself,
remember the refrain. I'm thinking abstain
but I'm singin' *Oklahoma.*

don't rant

we can agree to disagree

>we can't. we can't agree on anything so anything
>like agreement smells like appeasement and I'm buried
>in newsfeed and rubbish, rubbish that you pay to clear
>away like clockwork because you can and when
>your home is dressed in tryptophan and I burn turkey
>in the oven again—the most we can agree on is
>I need a slow-cooker and you rely on digital time

so we're good then

>we are not good and we are not done
>I was trying to keep it homespun I'll put it another way
>we cannot agree we should not agree we should
>resist this disease of our time, this bulldozing, this shame,
>this delusion, resistagree

it that a word?

>it's as good as any word it's called to stop it's called to fix
>it's answer to complacent, elixir to complicit,
>toxic, debilitating, heart-wrenching, gut-retching
>silence: silence as sickness
>insufferable, insatiable, inscrutable, out of control

now that sounds familiar

>it's no longer a choice
>it's not you say tomato or I go high
>or you go figure or I call it a day
>it's resistagree   resistagree

I heard you the first time

    you didn't and this is how we don't

THE HIDDEN MASTERPIECE BEHIND MISS AMY'S CONFIRMATION AND A NEW GENRE OF JUDICIAL PERFORMANCE ART

"Some of us will probably become famous. It will be an ironic fame fashioned largely by those who have never seen our work."
—Allan Kaprow, *Essays on the Blurring of Art and Life*

Welcome to *Miss Amy*, the newest installment of an art exhibition focusing on contemporary political figures:

Associate Justice of the Supreme Court, confirmed October 2020, 52–48

Due to the pandemic and these uncertain times, participants should wear face masks and refrain from screaming.

1: Echo Chamber with Strobe Light & Multiple Voices

Enter the small, dark room where teacher comments on report cards from St. Catherine's (elementary) flash on the ceiling. Words are recorded in surround-sound.

Miss Amy, you have mastered your craft, you will be rewarded on earth as it is in heaven. Miss Amy, go forth and multiply; the meek shall inherit the earth. Miss Amy, you have mastered Miss Amy you will be rewarded in heaven Miss Amy, go forth and multiply Miss Amy, inherit the earth.

2: Archive Room: Painting by Anonymous

Her eyes do not tell a story but her lips, thin and arrow straight, shoot right through the canvas. It appears that *Miss Amy* has mastered the art of non-expression. Her unbending posture contributes to an overall flat quality; observe that the body is not portrayed in any sort of abstract manner. This style is in direct contrast to contemporary art and especially the Neo-expressionists of the 70s, the subject's formative years.

3: Objects & Collectables

Note the important objects surrounding the subject (*Miss Amy*, Caucasian woman)

(A) Illuminated manuscripts: embossed with gold coin and silver filigree
(B) The Ceremonial Gavel: located on the far-right corner; made of a dark, heavy wood
(C) The Christ Child: fair infant swaddled in a blood-red blanket

The influence is Medieval Portraiture, where the goal is to present the subject *not* at a particular moment in time, but as the person wishes to be remembered. Objects represent *Miss Amy's* religious conviction and political position.

4: Jury Summation

It is tempting to dismiss *Miss Amy* as an example of bad art; art that has nothing new to offer, nothing interesting to bring to the table, art that is unchallenging and stale.

But despite an unremarkable aesthetic, the strength of *Miss Amy* lies in its lack of transparency, its *unknown futuristic quality*.

5: Heads in a Rose Garden

Observe the long row of doll heads in the final room, hung on a rectangular grass panel, surrounded by 200 plastic roses in a synthetic flower bed. To the left stands a single, 10-foot tall, pink-flowering crab apple.

This surreal doll and retro-toy collection, entitled *Heads of Fate*, is a nod to the various mindsets of *Miss Amy*. Red, white & blue wind-ups, pull-strings, spring toys and bobbleheads are pure mid-century.

It is important to note that *Miss Amy*, like most art commissioned by the civil government, courts, religious institutions and wealthy individuals, was created to communicate a message about the power of the patrons. *Miss Amy* was confirmed entirely by Patrons of her Art.

Pull the strings of these talking heads for a word from our sponsors:

"Squeeze me. I'm a technicality!"

"Separate-but-equal, wait for my sequel."

"Pull my trigger, not my mask."

"Don't laugh. I am not a joke."

PLEASE DISINFECT ON THE WAY OUT.

Stumped

Believe me, I believe you, candidate of order
law-breaking, shackles-off, hair-raising border-
line Mexican criminal deals made in China,
you do have a way with the random vagina

grabbing at truth as it plays on the news
high-wired penthouses trapping your muse
inspiring violence, hatred and dirt
slinging it back for a hot mini-skirt

But riddle me this: how do regular folk
watch you shoot from the hip just to swallow your joke?
Befuddled, bewildered, bewitched I am not
singing your praises or stirring your pot
of golden-white towers from armies of men
Ready, Aim, Fired
to tax us again

that second amendment my first-born should know
arms boys to be boys for stones that they throw
shatter glass ceilings, break family heart,
wrongs are not rights, they're rites torn apart

Let's dig through the mud and bury the lead,
God help us, brave homeland,
this sweet land of need

My Body in This Term

I am dead weight   waiting
gates or hell   freezer cell
expiration   organ donation
mourning veils   wails derails
my absent mind a digger's job
feared result   of angry mob
I am grounded   impounded
your wife   necrophilic life
burned ash   urned end

Common Shooting

On a mid-September afternoon
in historic Boston Common
        multiple gunshots were fired
near the bandstand, among bystanders, a brazen act
police called it, locals say this never happens in Boston,
        it's a college town.
A nineteen-year-old Hyde Park man
was critically injured. The shooting triggered
        chaos in one of the nation's oldest parks.
Police chased a man into a trolley tunnel at Arlington Station,
a gun was recovered, three are in custody.
        Police believe it was not a random act.
An argument preceded the shooting, all people involved
are known to police,
        it's unclear if it's drug or gang related.
But this is not about terrorists or homegrowns
or viable solutions for
        public safety.
This is about those who dodge a bullet—
        those who are not dead, yet

She calls me crying, barely able to speak, and I fear the worst.
Twenty minutes before, we had been chatting. She was
        on a mission to discover
a farmers' market. She loves her classes, her roommate.
I'm thrilled; this wasn't her first choice of schools.
        Please, God, don't let it be rape.
She tells me she ran from gunfire but she's safe, back in her dorm.
I'm relieved. School is on lockdown.
        On the internet. Looks like they caught the shooter.

She says she thought about playing dead instead of running.
We had discussed this right after Sandy Hook.
                Decades in New York, I've never run from gunfire.
Twitter says two of the three suspects fled on mopeds.
Impossible, she says. Those guys on the red Vespas were not the shooters.
                Are you sure you want to get involved?
She spent hours at police headquarters, couldn't sleep for days.
I flew her home for the weekend, took her shopping.
                Statistics say this shouldn't happen to her again.

But back to the Common. This story won't be found on CNN or Fox, The New York Times or Washington Post.
                It was just another boy
not enrolled in a college, somewhere in critical condition.
And three unnamed others, who knew each other and were known to police,
                released the next day.

this is what we mean by blue

my mother living near a tranquil sea
but caring for my father with dementia

blue-footed boobies dodging the recycle bags
are rarely blue, as they dance to mate,
lifting their feet in ecstasy

the cornflower sky I recall in my dreams
that afternoon we fell in love

a small butterfly landing soft on an iris
that reveals its gender only by its tone

the stiffness and the dread of war
as they blued the shirts
and starched the uniforms

that intermediate space between green and violet
the place we go when there's nothing more we can do

dim lights bluing the retina
help me see another side to the story

The Cardiologist

"It's human," he said, his eyes glancing away, as if he wanted to leave. "Oh," I said, and not much else. You're never ready for this diagnosis. Maybe I did say more. "I did nothing to deserve this."
He responded quickly. "Nobody does. It's part of being a person." He looked down at his notes before heading toward the exit.
"Wait," I said, stalling for time. Who should I blame? My mother came to mind, and her mother before her, and others in my genetic rolodex. Not to mention stress and fad diets.
It was absurd to argue, but I felt compelled.
"So what does this mean—I do nothing?"
Typical New Jersey doctor. I should have gone into the city.
"It's the condition," he said, handing me his notebook.
He left. I flipped through his blank pages,
making mental notes.

Unconventional Sonnet from a Party Girl

In a frenzied state we grab house seats
at our monthly caucus disguised as lunch.
You, my friend, choose presidential three-course
espousing on your glutton free
while I count empty calories lucky.
Pretense is our nation under God
divisible by the sum of those unfortunates
multiplied by calculated ladies who agree
to disagree as they divvy up the check.
Birthdays come and conventions go
to super delegated party chatter
primarily leading to swift completion
if snow or rain glooms decision day.
I vote we stay home and watch TV.

A 1980 Cruise

He was that Tom
but he could have been any Tom,
Dick or Harry, he was a regular guy,

a suburban kid,
Kentucky-bred polite
answering "yes ma'am,"

"yes sir," a certain attitude
I would call grateful,
even as a high schooler.

He played football
and Led Zeppelin with the other guys
but there was this one thing:

he danced disco—
when only the girls would dance disco,
he dared to go Travolta.

I remember once before a prom
he was dancing disco in the hall,
he took a turn with all the dates

and that smile, it was killer,
we had no idea
what was in store,

clanging weights down in the basement
with my brother
like he didn't have a plan—

I took him to audition in
New York, played piano
while he sang

Put on a Happy Face,
he shook every judge's hand
even after the ten-bar cut off.

"If they like you enough,"
he said as we left,
"they'll change the part for you,"

like there was no such thing as a *no*.
And this, I believe, sealed his fate.

To Nail Polish

I have read that the Queen of England will have none of it
but the Duchess of Sussex wore 'rose lounge' on her wedding day.
I myself love *black wicked* finished off with *girlie gloss*
as though my fingers sing *come, glisten to the music*

More subtle is *sheer nude,* but that only works if what's underneath is up to snuff. Sniff, not so much—nothing is worse
than a stiff whiff of varnish, vulgar! Flowers, flags and rainbows
are salon motifs painted on ticket booth operators and data system

inputters who spend their lives toiling in digital minutia, as if
their nails display shades of the real America. As for transparency,
the self-polisher uses *clear* to tighten her loose screw.
What to do with dried-up bottles impossible to open,

outdated titles by women destined to meet their metabolic end?
These are the stuff landfills are made of.

MIA

Yesterday I found myself at the counter of the universal
fingerprint agency because to teach kids you need to get
fingerprinted—digitally nowadays—I asked the clerk
if she was familiar with the word *adermatoglyphia*
then proceeded to tell her about the rare genetic disorder
that causes a person to have *no* fingerprints only
four known families have this condition—isn't that crazy?
I figured she'd be excited about it (this being her work
and all) but the conversation didn't go far—funny
when I first heard that word I was terribly excited
not just because I harbor a fantasy of living a life
of espionage but I also love discovering new words—
she smiled as if amused or perhaps she was fantasizing
about whole cities of persons missing their fingerprints

Colonizer

I am a city in a mountain of land
vast green country below
lifting my voice in cellular broadband

Saltwater pool where trees once fanned
filtration systems flow
I make cities of mountains and land

Burning a hole in silt and sand
smoky quartz homegrown
all in the service of cellular broadband

Buried are the sour pickles of man
indigenous spirits flown
I am sitting on mountainous land

I ask no person to lend a hand
I eat no more than what I've grown
human remains of cellular broadband

It's common to misunderstand
the urge to remain alone
I am a city in a mountain of land
lifting my voice in cellular broadband

Missing Key

The doors are locked and I'm searching for a way in.
I circle my house intent on finding a crack in the system
I painstakingly created, a loose bolt, a faulty window.
It's still light in Vermont but in one hour the sun will dip
behind the mountain, temperatures will fall, and I may still
be stuck outside, cursing. There are friends. There are neighbors.
Or I could resolve nothing, sit on the cool grass and wait.
On my iPhone, I view my furious attempts to break in
recorded on the outdoor cameras. There are family members
who hold a key, but rescues have never worked for me in the past.
I consider places for lost or hidden keys. They say gratitude is a
key. Solitude is a mountain. There are pines, cedars and hemlocks,
a range against the mango-magenta horizon,
a red-tailed hawk circling its prey.

About the Author

Heather Newman's poems appear in *Barrow Street 4x2, Hanging Loose Magazine, Wisconsin Review, Hole in Head Review, Matter, MoonPark Review, The Pi Review, Love's Executive Order, New Verse News, How to Love the World* (Storey Publishing), *Voices from Here, II* (Paulinskill Press), and more. Her work has been nominated for the Pushcart Prize.

Heather received her MFA in Creative Writing from The New School in 2019. She and her husband divide their time between New Jersey and Vermont.

www.ingramcontent.com/pod-product-compliance
Lightning Source LLC
Chambersburg PA
CBHW071230160426
43196CB00012B/2471